CINCINNATI BENGALS

ALL-TIME GREATS

BY TED COLEMAN

Book design by Jake Slavik
Cover design by Jake Slavik

Photographs ©: Kirby Lee/AP Images, cover (top), 1 (top); Owen C. Shaw/Icon Sportswire/AP Images, cover (bottom), 1 (bottom); Carl Iwasaki/Sports Illustrated/Getty Images, 4; Focus On Sport/Getty Images, 7; Focus On Sport/Getty Images Sport Classic/Getty Images, 8; Ron Vesely/Getty Images Sport Classic/Getty Images, 10; George Gojkovich/Getty Images Sport/Getty Images, 13; Focus on Sport/Getty Images Sport/Getty Images, 14; Al Messerschmidt/Getty Images Sport/Getty Images, 16; Stephen Dunn/Getty Images Sport/Getty Images, 19; Andy Lyons/Getty Images Sport/Getty Images, 21

Press Box Books, an imprint of Press Room Editions.

ISBN
978-1-63494-423-6 (library bound)
978-1-63494-440-3 (paperback)
978-1-63494-473-1 (epub)
978-1-63494-457-1 (hosted ebook)

Library of Congress Control Number: 2021916603

Distributed by North Star Editions, Inc.
2297 Waters Drive
Mendota Heights, MN 55120
www.northstareditions.com

Printed in the United States of America
012022

ABOUT THE AUTHOR

Ted Coleman is a sportswriter who lives in Louisville, Kentucky, with his trusty Affenpinscher, Chloe.

TABLE OF CONTENTS

TRUMPY
84
84

CHAPTER 1

BUILDING A SUPER BOWL TEAM

The Cincinnati Bengals played their first season in 1968. The team didn't win many games that year. But at least fans had tight end **Bob Trumpy** to cheer for. Many people consider Trumpy one of the first modern tight ends. That meant Trumpy could do more than block. He was also a great receiver. Trumpy ended his career with 4,600 receiving yards.

On defense, the Bengals had a strong secondary. Cornerbacks **Ken Riley** and **Lemar Parrish** led the way. Riley had a talent for making interceptions. He grabbed 65 of them during his 15 years with the Bengals. In fact, Riley has the fifth-most interceptions of all time.

Riley may have been the interception master, but Parrish was pretty good himself. He recorded 25 picks as a Bengal. Parrish could also return kicks. He had 13 return touchdowns in his career. Parrish made eight Pro Bowls thanks to his multiple skills.

In 1970, this core group of players led the Bengals to their first playoff appearance. The next year, quarterback **Ken Anderson** arrived. Anderson was a steady passer

STAT SPOTLIGHT

CAREER PASSING YARDS

BENGALS TEAM RECORD

Ken Anderson: 32,838

known for his accuracy. Thanks to Anderson, Cincinnati finally had a franchise quarterback. The Bengals just needed a few more players to become a top team.

One of Anderson's top weapons was wide receiver **Isaac Curtis**. Curtis was somewhat new to receiving when he joined the Bengals.

In his first two years of college, he had played running back. But Curtis had also been a sprinter in college, and the Bengals valued his speed. Curtis spent his entire 12-year career with Cincinnati. During that time, he recorded more than 7,100 receiving yards.

In 1976, linebacker **Reggie Williams** joined the Bengals defense. Williams was great in coverage. He notched 16 career interceptions. Williams was also a fierce pass rusher who racked up lots of sacks.

PAUL BROWN

Paul Brown is forever linked to the Cleveland Browns. That's the team he founded in the 1940s and coached for many years. But Brown also founded the Cincinnati Bengals. He served as Cincinnati's head coach from 1968 to 1975. When Brown died in 1991, his son Mike took over as the team's owner. In 2000, the Bengals opened their new stadium. They named it Paul Brown Stadium.

MUÑOZ
78

CHAPTER 2

EARNING THEIR STRIPES

In 1981, the Bengals started wearing their famous tiger-stripe helmets. They also emerged as one of the best teams in the National Football League (NFL). Their offensive line was a big reason why. Left tackle **Anthony Muñoz** was one of the greatest linemen of all time. And right guard **Max Montoya** was no slouch either.

The line's excellent blocking kept defenders away from the quarterback. That gave Ken Anderson plenty of time to find open receivers. And he made the most of it. Anderson won the

Most Valuable Player (MVP) award in 1981. That same season, Cincinnati made it all the way to the Super Bowl. However, the Bengals fell short in the big game. They lost to the San Francisco 49ers, 26–21.

Muñoz and Montoya also opened up holes for running back **James Brooks**. Brooks stood 5-foot-10 and weighed only 180 pounds. He didn't look like a star when the Bengals traded for him in 1984. But Brooks proved the doubters wrong. He had three 1,000-yard seasons and made four Pro Bowls. By the time Brooks left the Bengals, he was the team's all-time leading rusher.

Height was never a problem for wide receiver **Cris Collinsworth**. At 6-foot-5, Collinsworth's big frame helped him make big catches. As a rookie in 1981, he became

the team's first 1,000-yard receiver. He topped that mark three more times during his eight-year career.

In 1984, the Bengals drafted quarterback **Boomer Esiason**. The next season, Esiason took over as the starter. His arm was strong, but it was also accurate. In 1988, Esiason won the league's MVP award. More importantly, he led Cincinnati back to the Super Bowl. Unfortunately for Bengals fans, the team lost to the San Francisco 49ers once again.

THE ICKEY SHUFFLE

Fullback **Elbert "Ickey" Woods** played only 37 games for the Bengals. But his rookie season was one to remember. In 1988, he ran for 1,066 yards and scored 15 touchdowns. Woods is perhaps best known for his touchdown dance. It was known as the Ickey Shuffle. In truth, it wasn't much of a dance. Woods just hopped from side to side. The Ickey Shuffle may not have been pretty, but Bengals fans loved it.

The Bengals were more than just offense in the 1980s. Nose tackle **Tim Krumrie** was almost impossible to block. The defensive lineman recorded more than 1,000 tackles during his career. Meanwhile, safety **David Fulcher** made a name for himself with his hard hits on opposing receivers.

ANDERSON
71

CHAPTER 3
THE MODERN ERA

Bengals fans would never forget the memories of their Super Bowl era. But the players who made up those teams gradually retired in the 1990s. After that, the Bengals went into a period of decline. However, there was one thing that didn't change. Cincinnati still had some of the NFL's best offensive linemen.

Right tackle **Willie Anderson** faced many of the greatest pass rushers of all time during his 12 seasons with the Bengals. In three of those seasons, he didn't allow a single sack. Anderson made four straight Pro Bowls from 2003 to 2006.

Near the end of Anderson's career, the Bengals drafted left tackle **Andrew Whitworth**. Whitworth soon took over as a team leader.

Nobody had been able to top James Brooks's team rushing records until **Corey Dillon** arrived. Dillon racked up more than 1,000 rushing yards six seasons in a row. In 2000, he exploded for 278 yards in a single game. At the time, it was an NFL record.

Few Bengals sought more attention than wide receiver **Chad Johnson**. Most memorably, he changed his name to Chad

STAT SPOTLIGHT

CAREER RECEIVING YARDS

BENGALS TEAM RECORD

Chad Johnson: 10,783

Ochocinco for a few years. "Ocho cinco" is Spanish for "eight five." That was Johnson's uniform number. But Johnson wasn't just talk. He backed up his flashiness with productivity. Johnson became Cincinnati's all-time team leader in catches, receiving yards, and touchdowns.

A trio of Bengals legends made names for themselves in the 2010s. Quarterback **Andy Dalton** became Cincinnati's all-time leading passer. **A.J. Green** had the second-most receiving yards in Bengals history. And defensive end **Carlos Dunlap** became the team's all-time leader in sacks. These three players led Cincinnati to five straight playoff appearances between 2011 and 2015. But by the end of the decade, the Bengals were back in rebuilding mode.

Joe Burrow offered Cincinnati a reason for hope.

MARVIN LEWIS

Marvin Lewis coached the Bengals from 2003 to 2018. During that time, he won more games than any coach in Bengals history. But Lewis was better known for something else. He couldn't find a way to win in the playoffs. The Bengals lost in all seven playoff appearances they made under Lewis.

Burrow was the top draft pick in 2020. He was also an Ohio native. With Burrow at quarterback, Bengals fans dared to dream of another Super Bowl run.

TIMELINE

1968
1970
1980
1990
2000
2010
2020
BOB TRUMPY
(1968–77)
KEN RILEY
(1969–83)
LEMAR PARRISH
(1970–77)
KEN ANDERSON
(1971–86)
ISAAC CURTIS
(1973–84)
REGGIE WILLIAMS
(1976–89)
MAX MONTOYA
(1979–89)
ANTHONY MUÑOZ
(1980–92)
CRIS COLLINSWORTH
(1981–88)
JAMES BROOKS
(1984–91)
TIM KRUMRIE
(1983–94)
BOOMER ESIASON
(1984–92)
DAVID FULCHER
(1986–92)
WILLIE ANDERSON
(1996–2007)
COREY DILLON
(1997–2003)
CHAD JOHNSON
(2001–10)
ANDREW WHITWORTH
(2006–16)
CARLOS DUNLAP
(2010–20)
ANDY DALTON
(2011–19)
A.J. GREEN
(2011–20)
JOE BURROW
(2020–)

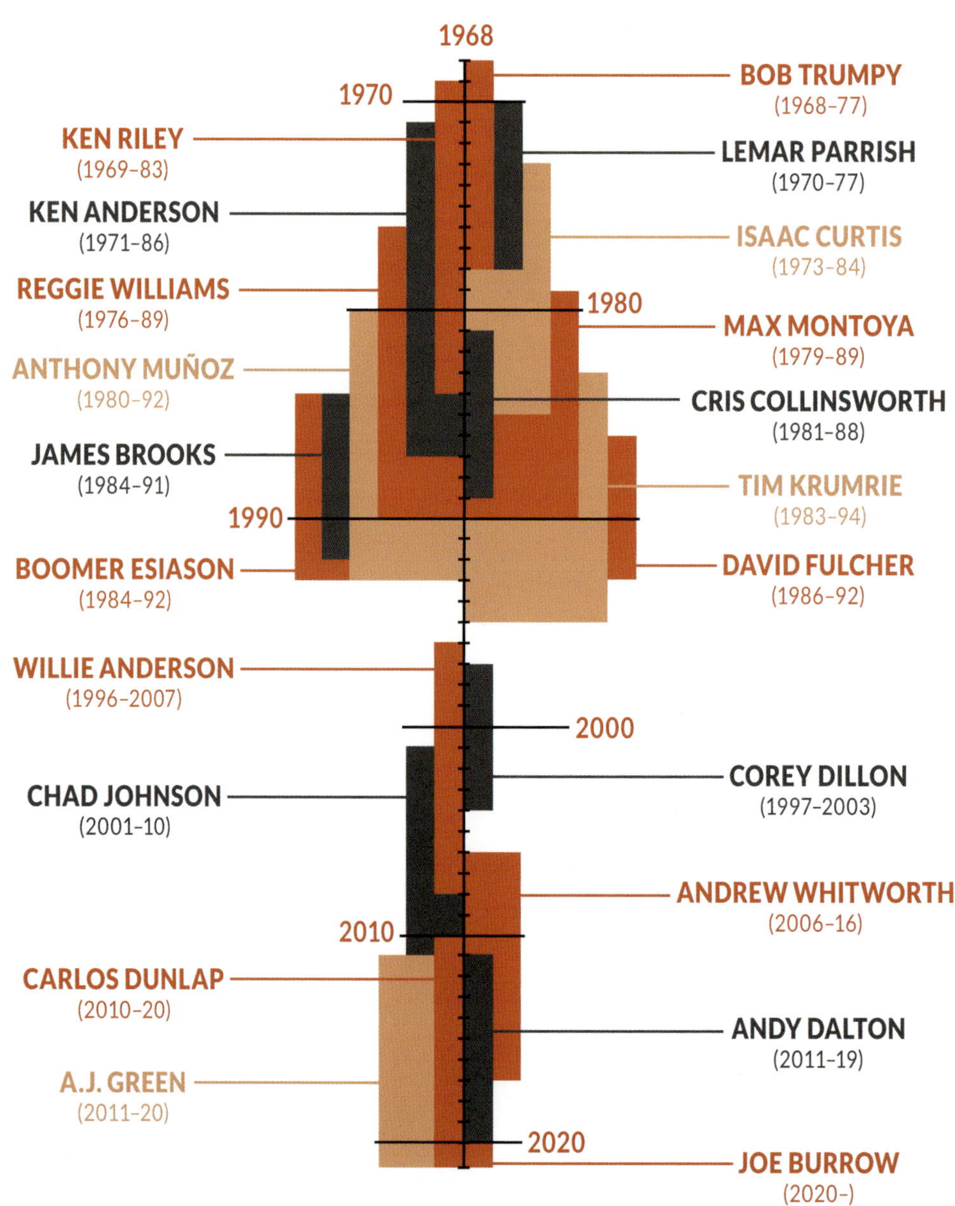

TEAM FACTS

CINCINNATI BENGALS

Founded: 1968

Super Bowl titles: 0*

Key coaches:

Forrest Gregg (1980–83), 32–25–0

Sam Wyche (1984–91), 61–66–0

Marvin Lewis (2003–18), 131–122–3

MORE INFORMATION

To learn more about the Cincinnati Bengals, go to **pressboxbooks.com/AllAccess.**

These links are routinely monitored and updated to provide the most current information available.

**1966 through 2020*

GLOSSARY

cornerback
A defensive player who covers wide receivers near the sidelines.

defensive end
A player who plays on either end of the defensive line and typically rushes the passer.

draft
An event that allows teams to choose new players coming into the league.

franchise quarterback
A quarterback capable of leading a team for a number of years.

linebacker
A player who lines up behind the defensive linemen and in front of the defensive backs.

rookie
A professional athlete in his or her first year of competition.

sack
A tackle of the quarterback behind the line of scrimmage.

secondary
The defensive players who typically cover wide receivers.

INDEX

NFL ALL-TIME GREATS

From the legends of the game to today's superstars, the National Football League has always been home to supremely talented players. This series introduces readers to the best of the best from their favorite teams through the years.

SPECIAL FEATURES:

- Informative sidebars
- Team facts
- Timeline
- Glossary
- Additional resources
- Index

READ ABOUT THE ALL-TIME GREATS FOR EACH OF THE 32 NFL TEAMS!

ISBN: 978-1-63494-440-3
90000
9 781634 944403